The Political Economy
of Intellectual Property Law

The Political Economy
of Intellectual Property Law

William M. Landes
and
Richard A. Posner

AEI-Brookings Joint Center for Regulatory Studies

WASHINGTON, D.C.

Available in the United States from the AEI Press, c/o Client Distribution Services, 193 Edwards Drive, Jackson, TN 38301. To order, call toll free: 1-800-343-4499. Distributed outside the United States by arrangement with Eurospan, 3 Henrietta Street, London WC2E 8LU, England.

Library of Congress Cataloging-in-Publication Data

Landes, William M.
    The political economy of intellectual property law / William M. Landes and Richard A. Posner.
       p. cm.
    Includes bibliographical references.
    ISBN 0-8447-7176-7 (pbk.)
       1. Intellectual property—Economic aspects—United States.
    2. Social choice—United States. I. Posner, Richard A. II. Title.

KF2979.L364 2004
346.7304'8—dc22

                              2004010290

10 09 08 07 06 05 04   1 2 3 4 5

The AEI Press
Publisher for the American Enterprise Institute
1150 17th Street, N.W.
Washington, D.C. 20036

Printed in the United States of America

Contents

Foreword

The 2002 AEI-Brookings Joint Center Distinguished Lecture Award was given to Richard Posner. The purpose of this award is to recognize an individual who has made major contributions to the field of regulation and related areas. Senior members of the Joint Center select the distinguished lecturer based on scholarly and practical contributions to the field. The lecturer is given complete latitude in choosing a topic for the lecture.

Judge Posner is one of the greatest original thinkers of our time. He has been and continues to be a towering intellectual giant in the field of law and economics—indeed, most scholars in the field learned from one of the editions of his pathbreaking textbook on the subject. In addition to making seminal contributions to the fields of regulation and antitrust, Judge Posner has written important works in a number of areas, including intellectual property, moral and legal theory, and law and literature.

This monograph, coauthored with Professor William Landes, focuses on the expansion of intellectual property law over the last half century. It first describes the expansion and then seeks to explain it. In so doing, it explores a fundamental, unresolved issue in the theory of regulation: why some kinds of regulation have increased dramatically over this period while others have virtually disappeared.

Like all Joint Center publications, this monograph can be freely downloaded at www.aei-brookings.org. We encourage educators to use and distribute these materials to their students.

ROBERT W. HAHN, Executive Director
ROBERT E. LITAN, Director
AEI-Brookings Joint Center
for Regulatory Studies

The Political Economy of Intellectual Property Law

William M. Landes and Richard A. Posner

The principal task we set for ourselves in this paper is to explain the expansion in intellectual property protection over the last fifty years or so and, in particular, the rapid growth that began, roughly speaking, with the 1976 Copyright Act. We also seek to understand why this expansion occurred in dissimilar ways across different types of intellectual property. To cite two examples, we find that the statutory expansion in copyrights has been more rapid than in either patents or trademarks, and that patent protection has grown in part as a result of the decisions of a court (which has no counterpart in other areas of intellectual property) that has exclusive jurisdiction over patent appeals.

The paper is organized as follows. Part I presents empirical evidence regarding the growth in intellectual property protection over the past fifty years. Part II reviews the theory of "public choice," which models the political and governmental process as the product of demand and supply factors, particularly the ability of interest groups to overcome free-rider problems. Part III applies public-choice theory to the growth and character of intellectual property protection.

This paper is an expanded version of a talk that Posner gave as an AEI-Brookings Joint Center Distinguished Lecture on November 19, 2002, which was based on chapter 14 of Landes and Posner, *The Economic Structure of Intellectual Property Law* (Harvard University Press, 2003).

1

I. The Growth in Intellectual Property Protection

A very crude measure of the expansion in intellectual property rights is the increase in the number of words in the principal intellectual property statutes, since most of those statutes expand such rights or create new ones rather than reduce existing rights. Figure 1 shows that the increase in words has been greatest for copyrights and lowest for trademarks. The copyright statute had 11,550 words in 1946, 22,310 in 1975, a tripling to 61,600 in 1976 with the passage of the new Copyright Act, and 124,320 words in 2000—a nearly elevenfold increase in fifty-four years. This translates into a 4.4 percent annual rate of growth and a 6.9 percent annual rate since 1975. The trademark statute (the Lanham Act) had 10,640 words in 1946, 13,345 in 1987, a jump to 20,136 in 1988 with the passage of the Trademark Revision Act, and 24,750 in 2000—a 1.4 percent annual growth rate. The patent statute had 24,565 words in 1946, 54,480 in 1976, and 110,880 in 2000—a more than fourfold increase since 1946, which translates into a 2.9 percent annual growth rate.[1]

Figure 1 also shows that these increases were not continuous but typically coincided with major statutory changes, such as the new Copyright Act in 1976, the Trademark Revision Act in 1988, and amendments to the Copyright Act in 1998 concerning digital copying and the copyright term. Also, in figure 1, we can estimate the relative growth in the intellectual property statutes by comparing the number of pages in the U.S. Code to the number of words in the intellectual property statutes.[2] The estimate is crude because the expansion in federal statutes reflects new areas of regulation (such as the civil rights laws) as well as amendments to existing laws. Moreover, additions to the U.S. Code include laws that reduce rather than increase the protection of property rights. For what they are worth, the data show that, between 1946 and 1994 (the last year for which we have the U.S. Code data), the size of the U.S. Code increased at an annual rate of 3.6 percent compared to 4.4 percent for copyright, 3.0 percent for patents, and 1.1 percent for trademarks.[3] Therefore, copyright is the only area of intellectual

FIGURE 1

INTELLECTUAL PROPERTY STATUTES AND U.S. CODE

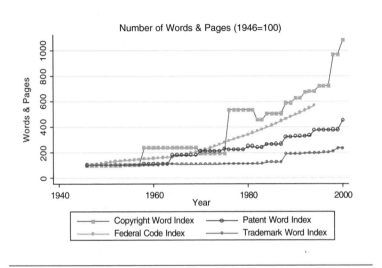

Number of Words & Pages (1946=100)

Copyright Word Index   Patent Word Index
Federal Code Index   Trademark Word Index

SOURCE: Authors' calculations.

property in which statutory expansion appears to be more rapid than the overall growth in federal statutes in the 1946–94 time period—although, as noted, the growth in federal legislation reflects both increases within established categories and new categories. The expansion in copyright was particularly rapid (7.9 percent) between 1994 and 2000, a period that includes two important amendments in 1998 to the Copyright Act—the Sonny Bono Copyright Term Extension Act and the Digital Millennium Copyright Act.

A related indicator of the recent expansion in intellectual property protection is the number of new laws and amendments enacted in the approximate quarter century since the Copyright Act of 1976, the first major revision of the copyright laws in the United States in nearly seventy years. The act added unpublished works to the category of covered works (thereby preempting common law copyright), significantly lengthened the copyright term, and added numerous provisions specifying the scope of protection for particular categories of work. The 1980s saw provisions added to deal with record rentals, semiconductors, and satellite transmissions, and to relax various formalities regarding notice and filing in order to bring our copyright law into compliance with the Berne Convention.

Trademark law also expanded in the 1980s. The Trademark Revision Act of 1988 created "an intent to use" system for registration that altered the long-standing principle that a trademark must be used in commerce before the owner can apply for registration. Yet, at the same time, the act weakened trademark protection by requiring that the use (which is required for actual registration, as distinct from the application for registration, the date of which would establish priority in a trademark dispute) be commercially significant and not merely a token use.

The most significant change in the patent area was the creation in 1982 of the U.S. Court of Appeals for the Federal Circuit to be the exclusive patent appellate court, in the expectation (about which more later) that it would interpret and apply the patent statute in a way that would strengthen inventors' rights.

In effect, judicial expansion of intellectual property rights was substituted for statutory changes, as indicated by the fact that a spline regression of the logarithm on the number of words in the patent statute indicates the rate of growth of words was actually greater in the period before than after 1982, although the difference is not statistically significant. The regression coefficients (and t-statistics) are 0.031 (14.2) for 1946–82 and 0.026 (7.4) for 1982–2000.

The legislative trend toward expanding the rights of intellectual property owners accelerated in the 1990s, with the enactment of such statutes as the Visual Artists Rights Act, the Architectural Works Protection Act, the Federal Trademark Dilution Act, the Anticybersquatting Consumer Protection Act, the Sonny Bono Copyright Term Extension Act, the Digital Millennium Copyright Act, and the ratification of the TRIPS (Trade-Related Aspects of Intellectual Property Rights) convention on international copyright protection.[4]

It may seem puzzling that more legislative activity occurred in the field of copyrights than in patents, since patents offer the potential of greater economic rents than copyrights; also puzzling is the lesser legislative activity regarding trademarks than either copyrights or patents. One factor, though limited to patents, is (as already mentioned) that Congress may have decided to delegate patent-protection expansion to the Federal Circuit. Another (though superficial) factor is that the copyright, patent, and trademark laws all have different structures. Copyright law tends to specify the nature of the protected work (for example, books), whereas patent and trademark law protect respectively inventions and brand names (or other signifiers of origin) more broadly. So, when new types of expressive works arise, such as sound recordings of computer software, or old types are thought in need of copyright protection, such as buildings as distinct merely from architectural plans, new legislation may be necessary to bring them under the copyright umbrella.

But this just pushes the question back to explaining the difference in the structure of the three bodies of law. One possibility is that patent and trademark statutes are drafted in more general terms (thus requiring less frequent amendment), because patents and trademarks are applied for rather than asserted. A filtering machinery, the proceeding before the Patent and Trademark Office, prevents the most questionable patent and trademark applications from being granted. In contrast, copyright is asserted. If the copyright statute defined copyrightable materials simply as "expressive works," the Copyright Office would have to expand its administrative proceedings to include a review of copyright applications for such things as originality, since otherwise there would be a great deal of litigation-fomenting confusion about which expressive works are validly covered by copyright and which are in the public domain. Statutory specificity substitutes for delegation to administrators (the staff of the Patent and Trademark Office) and judges (the Federal Circuit) at the price of requiring more frequent amendments.

Consistent with this suggestion, table 1 reveals significantly greater processing and administrative costs per patent and

TABLE 1

GOVERNMENT EXPENDITURES ON PROCESSING COPYRIGHT, PATENT, AND TRADEMARK APPLICATIONS

Costs	2000	2001	2002
Copyright			
Total	$37,485,014	$38,438,249	$40,896,000
Per registration	$72.70	$63.89	$78.48
Patent			
Total	$781,300,000	$882,500,000	$1,022,300,000
Per application	$2,506	$2,560	$2,902
Trademark			
Total	$130,000,000	$134,100,000	$138,700,000
Per application	$438	$576	$669
Application Fees			
Copyright			$30
Patent			$600
Trademark			$300

SOURCE: Patent and trademark program costs are found on p. 50 of the *Annual Report of the United States Patent and Trademark Office* in the section entitled "Results of Operations."
NOTES: (1) Trademark applications refer to the number of individual applications. There are, however, forty-seven different classes of items in which a trademark may be registered, and some individuals request registration in multiple classes. Total applications, including additional classes, are about 30 percent greater than individual applications. The per-application trademark uses individual applications not including application to register for additional classes of goods. (2) The patent fee is a weighted average of the $750 fee and $375 small entity fee with the weights equal to 0.6 and 0.4, respectively (based on the relative share of small entity applications).

trademark application than per copyright registration. The difference between patent and copyright is particularly striking. On average, the Copyright Office incurs a $70 cost per copyright registration, compared to about $2,500 per patent application and more than $3,500 per patent grant incurred by the PTO. This $2,400-plus differential between patents and copyrights reflects the time and effort required by the patent office to review the patentee's application to determine whether the invention satisfies the statutory requirements for a patent grant. Trademark expenditures per application fall between copyright and patent expenditures; they are roughly six to ten times greater than copyright expenditures but only about one quarter as great as patent expenditures. Like patents, a trademark is applied for rather than asserted, but the registration process is less demanding and hence involves lower administrative time and costs.[5]

Data on application fees for 2002 in table 1 provide further evidence on differences in the upfront costs incurred in acquiring property rights in intellectual property. Since the copyright, patent, and trademark offices are supported by user fees, we would expect differences in fees to correspond roughly to differences in the costs of servicing applications in these areas. Although these fees roughly track the estimated cost differences, patent fees appear low relative to copyright and trademark fees given the differences in cost; for example, the $600 patent fee is twice the trademark fee whereas the estimated cost per patent application in table 1 is about 4.8 times that of trademark applications.[6] The probable reason for the smaller initial fee difference between patents and trademarks is made up in the substantial additional fees that a patent holder must pay over the course of the patent term to maintain that patent in force. These include a fee of $1,300 when the patent is issued (the $600 fee is just for filing the application) plus maintenance fees of $890, $2,050, and $3,150 at 3.5, 7.5, and 11.5 years after the date of issue, respectively.[7] By comparison, a trademark owner pays a single $400 renewal fee twenty years after registration. Not surprisingly, postapplication fees generate almost twice as much revenue for the PTO as patent application fees, but only for about a tenth of the fees generated by trademark application fees.

Another administrative cost difference between patents and trademarks on the one hand and copyright on the other is that someone who believes that he will be harmed by a patent grant or trademark registration can bring an opposition proceeding before the PTO. Copyright law does not provide for opposition proceedings, since different parties can copyright identical works provided there was no copying of a copyrighted work. If one party alleges copying, the dispute is resolved in the federal courts rather than in an administrative hearing before the Copyright Office.

We can gain additional insight into why intellectual property rights have expanded in the United States by considering the growth in the underlying activities the statutes regulate. From a theoretical standpoint, we might expect a statute's length should be more or less invariant to the amount of activity regulated by it. Since a statute has an important public goods aspect to it, the cost of drafting a new provision should not depend on whether it covers 100 or 10,000 creators of intellectual property. We say "more or less" because growth in the underlying activity is likely to generate both greater heterogeneity in the activity itself and wealthier and more powerful interest groups that have greater stakes in the outcome of legislation (including groups that both favor and oppose the expansion of intellectual property rights). These factors tend to add new provisions and exceptions to the statute, which increase its length as the underlying activity expands. In addition, the average (as opposed to marginal) cost of drafting new provisions should decline as the number of intellectual property owners increases, because the total cost of new legislation is spread more widely.[8] Therefore, while we expect a positive relationship between statutory expansion and the level of the activity the statute regulates, this expansion may be slight if there are substantial economies of scale in the drafting of new statutory provisions.

The hypothesis that statutory activity and the activity regulated by the statute are positively correlated is supported by the data despite important differences among the categories of intellectual property. Since 1946, trademark registrations have grown more rapidly than either copyright registrations or patent grants: The annual rates are 0.034 (20.8) for trademarks, and 0.024 (27.5) and 0.022 (9.75) for copyrights and patents, respectively,[9] even though we know from figure 1 that the copyright statute expanded at a significantly higher rate (4.1 percent) than either the patent or trademark statutes (2.9 and 2.0 percent, respectively). Figure 2 reveals that the ratio of copyright registrations to words fell from a high of 20.6 in 1948 to a low of 4.1 in 2000, whereas the ratio of

FIGURE 2

RATIO OF REGISTRATIONS OR GRANTS TO WORDS

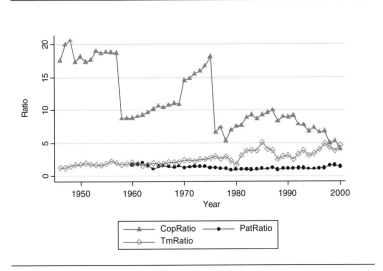

SOURCE: Authors' calculations.

trademark registrations to words increased from 1.3 in 1946 to 4.7 in 2000. In contrast, the ratio of patent grants to words remained largely unchanged.

Earlier we suggested that there may be less legislative activity in the patent area than in the copyright area because the structure of the patent law leaves more discretion to the courts, which today means primarily the Federal Circuit—a court that is hospitable to patent rights (more on this later)—with the result that patentees have less demand for legislative favor. (This point also tends to explain the amicus curiae statistics presented later in this paper, which reveal greater effort to obtain patent than copyright protection through the judicial process.) A similar argument may be available to explain why the trademark statute has not expanded in pace with the increase in registrations: The law is generally worded, leaving discretion to the courts, which have tended to exercise it favorably to intellectual property rights in general, including trademarks.

Another possible explanation for the greater legislative activity in the copyright field, though a weaker one and one in tension with our statistics, is that while *in principle* patents provide more legal protection and greater rent opportunities than copyright, the balance may have shifted because of the steps the law takes to curb that potential. These steps include making the patent term short (by copyright standards), requiring that the steps necessary to enable duplication of the invention be disclosed in the patent application, charging high maintenance fees, and making the patent applicant run the gauntlet of a PTO proceeding; in addition, there is the alternative of trade secrecy (rarely an alternative to copyright), which diminishes the demand for patent protection. As a result of all this, it is possible that today, given the very long copyright term and the very low costs of duplication of many types of copyrighted work (which would make the obtaining of rents from such work extremely difficult in the absence of copyright law), there are, in many areas, *greater* potential rents from copyright rather than patent protection.[10] But, if so, this leaves unexplained why patent holders have not obtained amendments to the statute that would give them rights more nearly equivalent to those that copyright holders now enjoy.

II. The Theory of Public Choice

Under the rubric of "public choice," economists try to explain legislation, and the political and governmental process more generally, by modeling government action as the result of the workings of demand and supply.[11] Particular emphasis is placed on the role of interest groups in overcoming the free-rider problem caused by the fact that legislation and policy are (for the most part) nonexcludable public goods. A person can enjoy the full benefit of the statute, regulation, or other policy in question without having contributed a dime to the collective effort necessary to get it promulgated.[12] This free-rider problem, like the parallel problem that besets cartelists (a seller that remains outside the cartel, undercutting the cartel price slightly, can increase its net profits, provided free riding does not destroy the cartel), can be overcome if the benefits of the collective effort required to get the legislation enacted are great and the costs either are small or, if large, are either widely diffused or imposed on politically impotent groups. These conditions are most likely to be satisfied if the legislation is backed by (but not opposed by) a compact interest group that has a lot to gain from the legislation.[13]

Public-choice theory has had only limited success in explaining political behavior and government action. Limited is not zero; the theory has made significant contributions to our understanding of public utility and common carrier regulation, certain other forms of regulation including occupational licensure and other labor-market (including safety and health) regulation, and tariffs. But it has not, for example, succeeded in explaining the forces that brought into being the system of property rights that is fundamental to a capitalist economy. Can it say anything about the extension of that system to encompass intellectual property and the spurt in intellectual property protection that we have dated to the 1976 copyright statute?[14] We find it helpful to approach the question by first considering another trend that began at roughly the same time: the deregulation movement.

Beginning in the late 1970s and continuing almost to the present day, a number of important industries in the transportation, communications (including broadcasting), energy, and financial-services (including banking) sectors—industries that until then had long been subject to comprehensive public regulation, mainly of the public utility or common carrier variety—were wholly or entirely deregulated. Significant partial deregulation occurred in other industries, including legal services. Probably the greatest success of public-choice theory has been in explaining the pattern of regulation that existed *before* deregulation took hold. Public-choice theory showed that the principal effect of such regulation was to bring about or shore up producers' cartels, and it identified the demand and supply factors that explained the success of some producers and the failure of others in obtaining such regulation. Those factors turned out to be much the same, as we have suggested, as the factors that facilitate purely private cartels. The more concentrated the cartelists' market and the more diffuse the buyer side of the market, the easier it is for the cartelists to overcome the free-rider problems that bedevil cartels—and if they can overcome those problems in the private marketplace, they may be able to overcome parallel problems in the political marketplace, where legislation is "bought." The main difference between private and regulatory cartels is that firms able to collude effectively without interference from antitrust authorities (as usually is the case if their collusion is tacit) have less demand for regulatory backing than firms facing greater obstacles to private cartelization. That is why, for example, farmers are more likely to seek legislation limiting agricultural competition than producers of cement are likely to seek regulation of the cement industry.

Public-choice theory has proved better at explaining regulation than at explaining deregulation.[15] But it can help us identify the factors that, taken together, may explain the latter phenomenon, though it cannot provide all the help we need.[16] One factor is the economic malaise of the 1970s, which created a demand for economic reform. That malaise, moreover, produced the election of Ronald Reagan, an economic liberal in the nineteenth-century sense—that is, a believer in free markets—and a magnet for other such believers, a number of whom received executive or judicial appointments. Even before that, with the election of Richard Nixon in 1968, free-market thinking had begun to take hold in the government. Though Nixon himself was not an economic liberal, some of his appointees were, to a degree anyway, including three of his four Supreme Court appointees (Burger, Rehnquist, and Powell). Another factor, and again one related to the economic distress (the "stagflation") of the 1970s, was the rise of the Chicago School of economic analysis. The most influential figure of the Chicago School was Milton Friedman, and his prestige and influence rose with the apparent failure of Keynesian economics, of which he was the leading critic.

These political and intellectual currents, though almost certainly one of the causal factors behind deregulation, might not have sufficed by themselves to bring about widespread deregulation.[17] But, in addition, many regulated firms were becoming restive under regulation. The high rate of inflation in the 1970s interacted with regulatory control over rates, and particularly the regulatory lag in granting rate increases, to impede needed pricing flexibility. Another factor, one solidly rooted in public-choice and cartel theory, was the tendency of cartelization (including cartelization by regulation) to transform cartel profits into costs. A cartelized market is not in equilibrium. Because the price exceeds the marginal cost of goods, there are unexploited profit opportunities. If price competition is prevented by agreement or regulation, the members of the cartel vie for additional sales by increasing the quality of their product until, at the margin, the cost of the product equals the price. At this point, regulation becomes all costs and no benefits, at least to the most efficient firms, whose expansion is inhibited by the protectionist philosophy of the regulators.[18]

III. Public Choice and Intellectual Property

Against this background, let us now consider the simultaneous trend toward ever-greater legal protection of intellectual property documented in Part I of this paper. Should intellectual property law be thought of as a form of regulation? In that case, the trend toward deregulation in other sectors of the economy was being bucked, as it were, by an equal and opposite regulation trend. That would not be a unique phenomenon; the regulation of health and safety, and of employment, increased during the era of deregulation, but those forms of regulation had begun well before the deregulation movement. Only the movement for greater protection of intellectual property actually coincided with the deregulation movement. We must try to explain this coincidence.

Analysis is complicated by the fact that the expansion of intellectual property has not been monotonic. A 1992 amendment to the fair use provision of the Copyright Act provided that the same general standard should govern the application of the fair use defense to unpublished as to published materials; in 1988 Congress (as mentioned in Part I) restored to the Lanham Act the requirement of commercially meaningful (rather than merely token) sales to establish trademark protection; the Trademark Clarification Act of 1984 established an implicit cost-benefit analysis for determining when a trademark has become a generic name; the anticybersquatting statute prevents an especially inefficient form of banking of trademarks; an amendment to the patent statute created a limited antitrust immunity for patent tie-ins; and the Hatch-Waxman Act expanded the experimental-use defense to patent infringement.[19] As explained in our book, all these seem to have been economically efficient legislative interventions into the existing body of intellectual property law.

Setting aside those interventions for the moment, let us consider whether there might be a public-choice explanation for what has undoubtedly been a net expansion of intellectual property rights. One factor is the inherent asymmetry between the value that creators of intellectual property place on having property rights and the value that would-be copiers place on the freedom to copy without having to obtain a license from the copyright holder or (in the case of patents) the inventor. The enforcement of an exclusive right to intellectual property can shower economic rents on the holder of that right, but copiers can hope to obtain only a competitive return. This should make it easier to organize a collective effort of copyright and patent owners to expand intellectual property rights than it would be to organize a copiers' interest group to oppose such an expansion. The music performing-rights organizations (mainly ASCAP and BMI) illustrate the ability of owners of intellectual property to organize coalitions to protect their ownership rights. It is noteworthy that "most of the statutory language" of the Copyright Act of 1976 "was not drafted by members of Congress or their staffs at all. Instead, the language evolved through a process of negotiation among authors, publishers, and other parties with economic interests in the property rights the statute defines."[20]

The asymmetry of stakes between originators and copiers of intellectual property becomes especially pronounced when, as has been true of every copyright law, an extension of the term of the intellectual property right is made applicable to existing works as well as those created after the extension. Since the costs of creating the existing works have already been borne, the additional revenue generated by the extension of their copyrights is almost entirely profit, that is, economic rent. In contrast, those opposing the extension do so on behalf of intellectual property that they have yet to create and that can be expected to yield them only a competitive return. So they have less to gain from a successful outcome to the struggle than the supporters of the extension.

On this theory, one might expect continuous, inexorable pressure from such owners to strengthen such rights. Tugging the other way, however, and thus helping explain the eddies in the flow of new rights-expanding statutes, is that most creators of intellectual property use intellectual property created by others as inputs into the creation of their own intellectual property. Any law that strengthens rights to such property beyond the level necessary to assure an adequate supply is likely to increase those input costs. This prospect may retard efforts by producers of intellectual property to press for expanding legal protection of such property; conceivably, it might even align the industry's interest with that of the society as a whole.

Consider for example whether businesses that value patent protection would prefer that the Patent and Trademark Office be lax in its review of patent applications or that it be strict. The obvious answer—lax—may be incorrect. If the PTO is known to be lax, courts will give less weight to the presumption of validity of patents; moreover, the makers of valuable inventions may find themselves impeded in obtaining patents by the existence of a large number of patents already issued in their area of research. So, again, the public and private interest in effective regulation of the patent process may coincide.

But this is unlikely to be a *general* feature of intellectual property law, because of the persisting asymmetry with regard to the private benefits from recognizing versus denying intellectual property rights. We have clues to the existence of this asymmetry in the absence of serious opposition to the bill that became the Sonny Bono Copyright Term Extension Act; in the difficulty that Professor Lessig encountered in finding a plaintiff to challenge the constitutionality of the act;[21] and in the fact that the Disney company was the strongest supporter of the act, even though many of its most successful characters and movies have been based on public domain works, such as *Cinderella* and *The Hunchback of Notre Dame*.[22] Disney faced the imminent expiration of its copyright on its original Steamboat Willie (Mickey Mouse) character; other owners of lucrative copyrights soon to expire were also strong supporters of extending the term. Copyright owners were generous contributors to House and Senate sponsors and supporters of the Sonny Bono Act. According to the Center for Responsive Politics, in 1996, television, motion picture, and music interests donated $1,419,717 to six of the act's eight sponsors and cosponsors: Spencer Abraham, Barbara Boxer, Dianne Feinstein, Orrin Hatch, Patrick Leahy, and Fred Thompson (information on donations to the other two, Howell Heflin and Alan Simpson, was not available). Disney, MCA, Viacom, Paramount Pictures, and Time Warner all donated conspicuously large amounts; for example, Disney gave $34,500 to Senator Leahy.[23]

One possible explanation for the asymmetry in stakes between copyright owners and public domain publishers is that the public domain really is not worth much—that we have been exaggerating the dependence of authors and inventors (especially the former) on previously created works. But this suggestion confuses private with social value. Public domain works have less private value than copyrightable works, because they cannot be appropriated. They may have great social value. It is true that most creators of expressive work do not want to appropriate any part of the public domain; they just want to incorporate some of it into their work without having to negotiate for a license. But the immediate effect of the Sonny Bono Act was not to remove anything from the public domain. It was merely to postpone the addition to the public domain of works on which the copyright would expire earlier were it not for the act. In effect, all the act did, so far as increasing the

os even in the expansion of that law in recent decades. Not
most dyed-in-the-wool public-choice theorist would be
eny that many laws serve the public interest or, more pre-
e a *conception* (quite possibly erroneous) of the public
her than the interest of some narrow interest group. Many
eorists would further concede that interest-group pres-
ot always necessary to procure the passage of efficient leg-
the formulation by judges of efficient common law rules.
o believe, for example, that interest groups are necessary
actment of laws protecting property rights or punishing
ehavior. If the benefit-cost ratio is high enough, collective
omes feasible, even in the absence of interest groups.
msetz, an economist distinctly unsympathetic to public
planations of legislation, nevertheless argued that the rise
 rights was due not to the machinations of interest groups
ag scarcity that had increased the value of property rights
the costs.[31] He did not propose a causal mechanism con-
erceived increase in the social benefits of a property rights
h its adoption via the political process but such theories
oseph Schumpeter's theory of democracy,[32] for example,
vie for office by offering voters attractive policies in much
way that sellers of ordinary goods vie for sales by offering
 attractive terms. If they fail to deliver, they may be voted
e, as happened to Jimmy Carter in 1980 and George Bush
he perceived ineffectuality of Democratic Party politicians
crime was a factor in the defeat of Democratic presidential
 in 1968 and the 1980s. If property rights and crime
n are important to enough voters, successful politicians
y these goods without the promptings or pressures of
oups. Mention of Carter is particularly apropos because his
 due in significant part to the "stagflation" of the 1970s.
 of expanding intellectual property rights argued that, by
 the pace of innovation, such an expansion would help to
nation out of the economic doldrums.
think about the history of intellectual property law
Middle Ages, we can, just as with Demsetz's theory of the

costs of future creators of intellectual property is concerned, was to
reduce the rate at which the public domain would expand.[24] The
expected private benefits of such expansion were likely to be small-
er than the expected private benefits of retaining copyright on
certain highly valuable properties, such as the Mickey Mouse character;[25] this may explain Disney's seeming, by its support of the
Sonny Bono Act, to be turning its back on the public domain, from
which it has derived such profit.

There is a sense in which the Sonny Bono Act is *too good*
an example of the asymmetry between the private value of intellectual property rights and the private value of the intellectual public
domain. Had the act been limited to expressive works created
after its date of passage, producers of intellectual property, such
as Disney, would have balanced the higher input costs resulting from
the prospective shrinkage of the public domain against the increased
revenue stream from a longer period of copyright protection, and
given discounting to present value, the trade-off would probably not
have favored the extension. Because the act applied to all existing
intellectual property as well, it conferred a windfall on owners of
existing intellectual property that distorted the balance. Compare
bankruptcy reform. *Ex ante*, debtors and creditors have a shared
interest in optimal bankruptcy law. If creditors have suboptimal
remedies against defaulting debtors, interest rates will be very high
and debtors as a whole will suffer. If creditors have excessively severe
remedies against defaulting debtors, people will be afraid to borrow,
and both the volume of and interest rates on loans will fall, to the
detriment of creditors. But *ex post*, debtors may benefit from a law
expanding bankruptcy exemptions or otherwise tilting the balance in
the law in favor of debtors, and creditors may benefit from the opposite tilt, because, in either case, the interest rate is fixed so far as cur-
rently outstanding credit is concerned. The possibility of retroactive
legislation is a candle to rent-seeking moths. This is a strong argument in favor of making legal reform prospective only, and it is as
applicable to intellectual property law as to bankruptcy law.

Sony's Betamax system[26] was a relatively rare example of a
product that had great commercial value, but only if intellectual

property protection was relaxed, as otherwise Sony would have owed enormous amounts of money in damages for contributory infringement. Having won its case, however, Sony and other producers of products bought to a considerable extent by infringers of intellectual property rights no longer had a strong incentive to seek legislative protection. In those situations in which concentrated economic interests would be adversely affected by expansion of intellectual property rights, such expansion is likely to be resisted effectively.[27]

An important example is the "passive carrier" exemption in the Copyright Act, which protects telecommunications companies from being sued for contributory infringement when they carry infringing materials, such as copyrighted music transmitted by infringers across the Internet.[28] The rampant piracy of copyrighted music and other copyrighted materials by users of the Internet has spurred a movement to limit the exemption, and this is a dispute that ranges interest groups on both sides of a controversy over the scope of intellectual property rights. The conflict between trademark owners and cybersquatters, resolved in favor of the former, is a similar example; another is the conflict between copyright owners and Internet service providers over "caching," resolved in the Digital Millennium Copyright Act in favor of the latter.[29]

An even better example, because it relates directly to the Sonny Bono Act, concerns the fees that ASCAP and BMI charge restaurants and other retail establishments for a blanket license to play the copyrighted music controlled by these organizations. Passage of the act was stymied until a provision excusing restaurants, bars, and other retailers of limited square footage from having to pay the license fee for recorded music broadcast on their premises was written into it.

A further consideration of a public-choice character, this one also discernible in the legislative history of the Sonny Bono Act, is mercantilist. The United States has a very large positive balance of trade in intellectual property. This means that the access costs imposed whenever intellectual property rights are enforced are shifted in part to foreigners, who neither vote in nor are permitted

to make campaign contributions in U… tries have often obtained special p… government. Mercantilism to one s… United States, has a comparative adv… tual property is more likely to favo… than one that does not.

We have tried to get an angle on th… formulation of intellectual property lav… briefs in the Supreme Court in intellec… an amicus curiae brief can be filed by a… organizations and most individual file… organizations. Hence, amicus curiae … interest-group activity. Since 1980, t… June 2003) decided thirty-three intell… sented substantive issues of intellectu… amicus curiae briefs were filed. A tot… supporting or opposing intellectual pr… these cases[30]—and, as we would ex… intellectual property rights. However,… the eleven patent cases in the sampl… were filed in support of patent pr… against. In the other twenty-two cases… support of the intellectual property ri…

By way of comparison, in the th… Supreme Court since 1980 in which… law were presented and amicus curia… of the amicus briefs supported a find… been violated and ninety-six oppo… with the statistics on amicus briefs in… indicates less support among filers… "rights" than for intellectual propert… because the period since 1980 has b… of antitrust liability has contracted… intellectual property, expanded.

We must not ignore the possib… public interest component in intelle…

and pe…
even t…
likely t…
cisely,…
interest…
of thes…
sures a…
islation…
It is ha…
for the…
crimina…
action…
Harold…
interest…
of prop…
but to r…
relative…
necting…
system…
exist. In…
politicia…
the sam…
consume…
out of o…
in 1992.…
to repres…
candidat…
suppress…
will sup…
interest g…
defeat w…
Advocate…
increasir…
bring the…
If w…
since the…

emergence of property rights in physical property, easily tell a "Whiggish" (history as progressive) story, in which the growth of intellectual property rights is explained by reference to material and social changes that increased the social value of such rights. When copying is expensive relative to the cost of expression—and here we add, bringing inventions into the picture, when duplicating an invention is expensive relative to the cost of developing the invention—the value of intellectual property rights is limited; authors and inventors do not need them in order to be protected from copying that is so fast and cheap that it prevents them from recovering their fixed costs of expression or invention. The expansion of trademark rights over the past century can also be explained as a response to market forces. With the reduction in transportation costs and the growth of specialization in markets, buyers have less and less contact with sellers or information about them. In such markets, trademarks provide consumers with an economical means of acquiring information on the reputation of sellers and the quality of goods sold. A reinforcing factor in the overall expansion of intellectual property is that such rights tend to be costly to define and enforce. These costs are likely to be particularly high in an unsophisticated legal system.

As the system becomes more sophisticated in the sense of better able to resolve disputes that involve difficult issues (such as whether two expressive works are substantially similar or whether a new invention duplicates an old one), as the cost of copying falls and its speed increases as a consequence of technological developments, as moreover technological progress becomes more highly valued and originality in general more highly prized, the costs of intellectual property rights fall and the benefits rise, leading us to expect intellectual property rights to expand even in a political regime oriented toward promoting the public interest. By the time the U.S. Constitution was drafted in 1787, twelve of the thirteen states had already adopted copyright laws, and common law patents were widely recognized. The Constitution's grant of power to Congress to enact national patent copyright laws was uncontroversial, and patent and copyright statutes were passed by the first

Congress.[33] The parallel to the rise of rights over physical property and the concomitant decline of common property is apparent. It is interesting to note in this connection that developing countries gave their (grudging) assent to the World Trade Organization Agreement on Trade-Related Aspects of Intellectual Property Rights (TRIPS), which greatly strengthened the international enforcement of intellectual property rights, in part because they anticipated such benefits as a greater willingness by the developed countries to transfer technology to them and a greater spur to production of intellectual property by their own enterprises.[34]

But the history we are recounting, while it might explain the enactment of the Digital Millennium Copyright Act in response to technological advances that make exact copying of digital files virtually costless and virtually instantaneous as well, does not explain why 1976 should be an inflection point, marking the beginning of a sudden and unprecedented growth in the legal protection of intellectual property in general. If, however, we consider carefully the political and ideological forces that were about to precipitate the deregulation movement, we shall discover some clues to a possible answer. Free-market ideology is friendly to property rights. In extreme versions of that ideology, the goal of economic liberalism is total commodification—everything of economic value owned by someone. Even short of this, an important and worthwhile goal of the deregulation movement was to substitute, so far as possible, market-based solutions to economic problems for solutions based on direct regulation. "Free-market environmentalism" proposed that conservation of scarce natural resources, whether ocean fisheries or the electromagnetic spectrum, could be achieved most efficiently by broader recognition of property rights, while pollution could be best controlled by such market-oriented, rights-based measures as tradable permits for the emission of pollutants such as sulfur dioxide.[35] Markets and property rights go hand in hand. Property rights provide the basic incentives for private economic activity and the starting point for transactions whereby resources are shifted to their most valuable use.

Given the historically and functionally close relation between markets and property rights, it was natural for free-market ideologists to favor an expansion of intellectual property rights. Natural— and it would have been clearly right either if intellectual property rights had identical economic properties to physical property rights, which however they do not, or if a system of direct regulation of expressive and inventive activity had been in place and the proposal had been to substitute a system based on property rights. If, in 1976, there had been no patent system but instead a system of direct government awards to successful inventors or direct government financing of R&D by private companies; if royalties in licenses of intellectual property had been fixed by the government rather than by contract; if the publication of books had been a government monopoly; if the prices of books, drugs, and other goods that embody intellectual property were fixed by a regulatory agency; if, to minimize access costs, intellectual property was given away for free and its costs subsidized by the government—if any of these things had been true—substitution of patent and copyright and trade secret and trademark law, in short, of intellectual property rights, would have been a step in the right direction from the standpoint of economic efficiency and a major plank in the platform of the deregulation movement. But none of these things *was* true. Intellectual property was already "deregulated" in favor of a property rights system, and the danger that the system would be extended beyond the optimal point was as great as the danger that it would be undone by a continuing decline in the cost (especially the quality-adjusted cost) of copying.

Equating intellectual property rights to physical property rights overlooks the much greater governmental involvement in the former domain than in the latter, at least in a mature society in which almost all physical property is privately owned, so that almost all transactions involving such property are private. Government is continuously involved in the creation of intellectual property rights through the issuance of patents, copyrights, and trademarks. Skeptics of government should hesitate to extend a presumption of efficiency to a process by which government grants rights to exclude competition with the holders of the rights. Friedrich Hayek, than whom no stronger defender of property rights can easily be imagined, warned that "a slavish application [to intellectual property] of the concept of property as it has been developed for material things has done a great deal to foster the growth of monopoly and . . . here drastic reforms may be required if competition is to be made to work. In the field of industrial patents in particular we shall have seriously to examine whether the award of a monopoly privilege is really the most appropriate and effective form of reward for the kind of risk-bearing which investment in scientific research involves."[36]

Another political factor in the sharp increase in the scope of intellectual property protection that we are dating from 1976 was the belief that one of either the causes or consequences of the economic malaise of the 1970s was a decline in the competitiveness of U.S. industry attributable to a loss of technological momentum to competing nations, notably Japan. This became a rationale for increasing patent protection through creation of a court that would have exclusive jurisdiction over patent appeals, although of course Japanese and other inventors would be free to seek U.S. patents. The system of patent appeals that preceded the creation of the Federal Circuit may actually have caused a decline in the number of patents issued, after correction for other factors;[37] some inkling of this may have played a role in the creation of the court, given the widespread concern about the rate of U.S. technological progress. The expansion of intellectual property rights was also doubtless propelled by a desire to alleviate our chronic trade deficits by increasing the income of owners of copyrights and other intellectual property, most of those owners being American.

Earlier we mentioned Nixon's Supreme Court appointments. These appointees found the economic critique of traditional antitrust policy persuasive. And so, during the 1970s and 1980s, the Supreme Court, joined in the Reagan years by the Department of Justice and the Federal Trade Commission, backtracked from the antitrust hawkishness of previous decades. One component of that hawkishness had been hostility to intellectual property rights, which were viewed as sources of monopoly power (which they are, but rarely to a degree having any antitrust significance). So the shift in antitrust policy, as well as increased favor for property rights, created an increasingly hospitable climate for intellectual property rights.

Whether the increases in the legal protection of intellectual property since 1976 have conferred net benefits on the U.S. economy is uncertain. But the political forces and ideological currents that we describe, abetted by interest-group pressures that favor originators of intellectual property over copiers, may explain the increases. An additional factor is the growth in the market for intellectual property. That growth cannot be dated to 1976; but there is no doubt that recent decades have seen a marked growth in that market, as the economies of the advanced nations shifted from "industrial" economies to "information" economies. That growth increased the potential economic rents from intellectual property rights and so may have increased the asymmetry of incentives that we have been stressing between supporters and opponents of expanded intellectual property rights.

The analysis is further complicated, however, by the fact that legal policy toward intellectual property rights is shaped by judicial as well as legislative action. Public-choice analysis focuses on legislation, because the play of interest groups in the legislative process is widely acknowledged and it thus becomes plausible to view legislation as a product demanded by and supplied to influential interest groups in exchange for political support, including campaign contributions. The judicial process, in contrast, is structured to minimize the role of interest groups; interest groups can file amicus curiae briefs, but judges have little incentive to give much weight to such briefs. For these and other reasons, economic analysis of legal institutions has tended to distinguish between common law and legislative policymaking and to argue that the former is, for a variety of reasons including judicial incentives and constraints, more likely than the latter to be economically efficient.[38] We find this pattern in intellectual property law as well, to a considerable extent though not completely. The most efficient areas of intellectual property law appear to be the largely common law fields of trademark, trade secrecy, and publicity rights law,[39] plus common law copyright and the very important doctrine of fair use in copyright law—still largely common law although codified in the Copyright Act of 1976. Similarly, though the vitally important nonobviousness requirement of patent law was not codified until the Patent Act of 1952, judges had long been invalidating patents for obviousness. On the whole, then, the judge-made parts of intellectual property law seem pretty efficient; it is not the judges who are to be blamed for setting the copyright and patent terms, abolishing copyright renewals in favor of a single very long term, importing the "moral rights" doctrine into the copyright statute, or making buildings as well as building plans copyrightable. As in previous economic analysis of judge-made law, our book notes numerous instances of economic ingenuity displayed in judge-made rules and judicial decisions.

Because of the role the Federal Circuit has played in expanding patent protection, explaining why the legal protection of intellectual property protection has been expanding in recent decades requires consideration of the distinctive political economy of specialized as distinct from generalist judges. Not that the Federal Circuit is completely specialized; its jurisdiction ranges well beyond patent cases. Nevertheless, patent cases are the most important part of its jurisdiction, and a specialized court is more likely to have a "mission" orientation than a generalist court. That has been the experience with the Federal Circuit; it has defined its mission as promoting technological progress by enlarging patent rights.

This, in turn, suggests a possible public-choice explanation for the creation of that court. In other work, we have found that the creation of the court was responsible for an increase in the number of patents applied for and granted, but we have not found that the increase has had a positive effect on the rate of technological progress.[40] The most certain effect of the creation of the court has been to increase the demand for the services of patent lawyers, a demand positively related to the number of patents granted, for that number in turn induces an increased number of patent applications, all of which require lawyer input. And the patent bar pressed strongly for the new court, though there was some internal tension owing to the fear by patent lawyers outside of Washington, D.C., that the centralization of patent appeals in Washington would give the D.C. patent bar a competitive advantage.[41] The creation of the court, whose specialized character and resulting "mission" orientation enabled a prediction that it would favor patents more than the generalist federal appellate courts, may thus have been a consequence largely of interest-group politics.

Notes

1. A regression of the logarithm of words on time yielded annual rates of growth (*t*-ratios in parentheses) in the 1946–2000 period of 0.044 (21.7) for copyrights, 0.014 (11.63) for trademarks, and 0.029 (23.54) for patents. All the differences in these growth rates are highly significant.

2. The data on the number of pages are from Figure 2 in Gary S. Becker and Casey Mulligan, "Accounting for the Growth in Government" (University of Chicago Department of Economics, April 2000).

3. We regressed the logarithm of pages or words on time. All regression coefficients are highly significant (*t*-statistics range from 8.5 to 62.6), and the differences among the estimated growth rates are also statistically significant.

4. A spline regression of the logarithm of the total number of words in patent, copyright, and trademark statutes on three time variables (1958–76, 1976–90, and 1990–2000) yields coefficients of 0.31 (10.7), 0.31 (9.1), and 0.37 (6.0) on the year variables, indicating a higher (though not statistically significant) rate of growth in the 1990–2000 period than in the earlier periods.

5. In trademarks, the examiner determines if the applicant's mark is used in commerce, is distinctive and not merely descriptive, and is not likely to cause confusion with other registered marks, not whether the applicant has a right to use the mark or use it exclusively. In contrast, the patent application takes considerably longer, the applicant is typically represented by an attorney, and the examination considers evidence on whether the invention is new, not obvious, and useful.

6. This understates the trademark application fee per applicant, since each trademark application covers on average 1.4 product classes. Since the application fee is for a single product class, each applicant pays on average $420 (= $300 × 1.4).

7. There is a 50 percent discount on all these fees for small entities.

8. This assumes that interest-group members are "charged" an average cost (or a multiple of an average cost) to cover the group's cost of organizing and supporting new legislation and that the marginal benefit to an

individual from new legislation does not decline as the size of the interest group grows. If, for example, both the marginal benefits and average cost declined proportionately as the group expanded, the interest group would not commit additional funds to press for new legislation.

9. Growth rates are estimated from logarithmic regressions and t-statistics are in parentheses. Data on trademarks and copyrights are from 1946 to 2000, whereas data on patent grants are from 1960 to 2000. Trademark and copyright growth rates from 1960 to 2000 (0.042 and 0.025) are about the same as in the 1946–2000 period. The differences between the growth rates for trademarks and copyright and trademarks and patents are highly significant at the 0.001 level, while the difference between copyright and patents is insignificant.

10. A point cutting the other way, however, is that, with more and more direct selling to consumers (for example, of software), owners of intellectual property can use contract law to protect their property and do not need to rely on copyright law. Copyright law is important where the would-be copier has no contractual relation with the copyright owner because he has purchased the copyrighted work from a retail store or other middleman.

11. For useful summaries of public-choice theory, see Robert D. Cooter, *The Strategic Constitution* (2000); Daniel A. Farber and Philip P. Frickey, *Law and Public Choice: A Critical Introduction* (1991); Jonathan R. Macey, "Public Choice and the Law," in *The New Palgrave Dictionary of Economics and the Law*, vol. 3, p. 171 (Peter Newman ed. 1998).

12. In contrast, intellectual property is an excludable public good.

13. On the role of interest groups in public policy, see, for example, George J. Stigler, *The Citizen and the State: Essays on Regulation* (1975); Stephen P. Magee, William A. Brock, and Leslie Young, *Black Hole Tariffs and Endogenous Political Theory: Political Economy in General Equilibrium* (1989); Richard A. Posner, "Theories of Economic Regulation," 5 *Bell Journal of Economics and Management Science* 335 (1974).

14. These are not the only questions about intellectual property law that public-choice theory might be able to shed light on. Josh Lerner, "150 Years of Patent Protection," 92 *American Economic Review Papers and Proceedings* 221 (May 2002), finds that patent protection is greater in wealthier and more democratic countries than in poorer and less democratic ones. Wealthy countries are more likely to be producers as well as consumers of intellectual property, creating a demand for intellectual property protection; and democratic countries are more hospitable to innovative thinking than less democratic ones.

15. As argued in Steven K. Vogel, *Freer Markets, More Rules: Regulatory Reform in Advanced Industrial Countries*, chapter 1 (1996).

16. For an excellent discussion, see Organisation for Economic Co-operation and Development (OECD), *Regulatory Reform in the United States* 18–20 (1999).

17. See Martha Derthick and Paul Quirk, *The Politics of Deregulation,* 245–46 (1985).

18. See id. at 19–20; Joseph D. Kearney and Thomas W. Merrill, "The Great Transformation of Regulated Industries Law," 98 *Columbia Law Review* 1323, 1394–97 (1998). "All costs and no benefits" is something of an exaggeration, however, since if the marginal cost of nonprice competition slopes steeply upward, the total costs expended on that competition may not be great. See George J. Stigler, "Price and Nonprice Competition," in Stigler, *The Organization of Industry* 23 (1968).

19. For citations and discussion, see Landes and Posner, note 1 earlier, chapters 4, 7, and 11.

20. Jessica D. Litman, "Copyright, Compromise, and Legislative History," 72 *Cornell Law Review* 857, 860–61 (1987).

21. See Steven Levy, "The Great Liberator," *Wired,* October 2002, 140, 155. Lessig was the lead counsel for the plaintiff in *Eldred v. Ashcroft,* 123 S. Ct. 769 (2003), the case in which the Supreme Court upheld the act's constitutionality.

22. See Robert P. Merges, "One Hundred Years of Solitude: Intellectual Property Law, 1900–2000," 88 *California Law Review* 2187, 2236 n. 219 (2000); Chris Sprigman, "The Mouse That Ate the Public Domain: Disney, the Copyright Term Extension Act, and *Eldred v. Ashcroft,*" *Findlaw's Writ,* http://writ.news.findlaw.com/commentary/20020305_sprigman.html (visited June 16, 2002); Daren Fonda, "Copyright's Crusader," *Boston Globe Magazine,* August 29, 1999, http://www.boston.com/globe/magazine/8 29/featurestory1.shtml (accessed July 3, 2003).

23. See http://www.opensecrets.org/politicians/candlist.asp?Sort= N&Cong=104 (visited July 3, 2003); see also Michael H. Davis, "Extending Copyright and the Constitution: Have I Stayed Too Long?" 52 *Florida Law Review* 989, 998–99 (2000)

24. In the limit, a twenty-year extension in the copyright term would freeze the size of the public domain for twenty years, then it would grow at the rate it would have grown twenty years earlier. During this twenty-year interval, copyrights on works that would have entered the public domain continue to earn royalties.

25. See Merges, note 22 earlier, at 2236–37.

26. See *Sony Corp. of America v. Universal City Studios, Inc.,* 464 U.S. 417 (1984).

27. See Merges, note 22 earlier, at 2237–38.

28. See 17 U.S.C. § 111(a)(3).

29. *Caching* refers to the temporary copy that an Internet service provider makes of transmitted material on a local server so that the subscriber can, after looking at the material, look at it again by clicking "Back" on a browser rather than by having to get it transmitted via long distance from the original sender.

30. A list of the cases is available from the authors.

31. See Harold Demsetz, "Toward a Theory of Property Rights," 57 *American Economic Review Papers and Proceedings* 347, 350–53 (May 1967).

32. See Joseph A. Schumpeter, *Capitalism, Socialism, and Democracy*, chapters 22–23 (1942), reprinted as chapter 9 of *Political Philosophy* (Anthony Quinton ed. 1967). For a summary of his theory, see John Medearis, *Joseph Schumpeter's Two Theories of Democracy* (2001); for an elaboration of it, see Richard A. Posner, *Law, Pragmatism, and Democracy*, chapters 4–6 (2003).

33. See Bruce W. Bugbee, *Genesis of American Patent and Copyright Law* (1967); Frank D. Prager, "Historic Background and Foundation of American Patent Law," 5 *Journal of Legal History* 309 (1961); Irah Donner, "The Copyright Clause of the U.S. Constitution: Why Did the Framers Include It with Unanimous Approval?" 36 *American Journal of Legal History* 361 (1992).

34. See Duncan Matthews, *Globalising Intellectual Property Rights: The TRIPS Agreement*, chapter 5 (2002). Evidence concerning these and other benefits of intellectual property rights protection to developing countries is summarized in Keith E. Maskus, "Intellectual Property Rights and Economic Development," 32 *Case Western Reserve Journal of International Law* 441, 478–88 (2000).

35. See, for example, Terry L. Anderson and D. R. Leal, *Free Market Environmentalism* (1991); Symposium, "The Law and Economics of Property Rights to Radio Spectrum," 41 *Journal of Law and Economics* 521 (1998); Elisabeth Krecké, "Environmental Policies and Competitiveness," 16 *Homo Oeconomicus* 177 (1999). For other references, see Elinor Ostrom, *Governing the Commons: The Evolution of Institutions for Collective Action* 12–13 (1990).

36. Friedrich A. Hayek, *Individualism and Economic Order*, 114 (1948).

37. See Landes and Posner, *The Economic Structure of Intellectual Property Law*, chapter 12.

38. This was a principal theme of our book *The Economic Structure of Tort Law* (1987). See also Richard A. Posner, *Economic Analysis of Law* (6th ed. 2003), especially part 2, and *Frontiers of Legal Theory*, chapter 1 (2001). The term *common law* requires definition, however. In its narrowest sense, it refers to the bodies of law administered by the common law courts of England in the eighteenth century and thus excludes admiralty law, domestic relations law, and equity jurisprudence. In a broader sense, it refers to

any body of law that is judge created. In its broadest sense, and the one in which we use it in this book, it refers not only to judge-created bodies of law but also to judge-created doctrines that fill gaps or resolve ambiguities in statutes or constitutions. In this sense, much of antitrust law, much of constitutional law, and much of patent and copyright law are common law. As mentioned in the text, several areas of intellectual property law are common law in the second sense as well, statutes being absent or merely codifications of common law principles.

39. The main trademark statute, the federal Lanham Act, is quite detailed, but many of its most significant provisions merely codify judge-created doctrines, such as functionality, 15 U.S.C. § 1053(e)(5), or the nontransfer-ability of a trademark "in gross," that is, without the assets for making the trademarked product. Id., § 1060.

40. See Landes and Posner, chapter 12; and our article "An Empirical Analysis of the Patent Court" (forthcoming in *University of Chicago Law Review*).

41. See Cecil D. Quillen, Jr., "The U.S. Patent System: Is It Broke? And Who Can Fix It If It Is?" 18–19 (unpublished, May 11, 2001); Quillen, "Innovators, Innovation, and the U.S. Patent System" 7–10 (unpublished, October 17, 2002).

About the Authors

William M. Landes is the Clifton R. Musser Professor of Law and Economics at the University of Chicago Law School, where he teaches economic analysis of law, art law, and intellectual property. He received his PhD in economics from Columbia University. Before joining the faculty of the University of Chicago Law School, Dr. Landes taught in the economics departments of Stanford University, Columbia University, and the Graduate Center of the City University of New York. He specializes in the application of economics to legal problems and has written widely in the fields of torts and antitrust. Formerly the president of the American Law and Economics Association, Dr. Landes has appeared as an expert before courts, administrative agencies, and committees of Congress. He is coeditor of the *Journal of Legal Studies*.

The Honorable Richard A. Posner was appointed to the U.S. Court of Appeals for the Seventh Circuit in 1981, and served as the chief judge from 1993 to 2000. Prior to his appointment, Judge Posner taught at the University of Chicago Law School for twelve years; earlier he had held several positions in Washington, including law clerk for U.S. Supreme Court Justice William J. Brennan Jr., assistant to the Solicitor General Thurgood Marshall, and general counsel of President Johnson's Task Force on Communications Policy. Judge Posner's contributions to the field of law and economics, like the many honors he has received, are too numerous to be listed. He is the author of the landmark *Antitrust Law* (2d ed. 2001), as well as *Economic Analysis of Law* (6th ed. 2003), and the founder of the *Journal of Legal Studies*.

JOINT CENTER